# Counterpoints

Paired Sources from U.S. History,
1877-present

Edited by Jonathan Rees

# Counterpoints: Paired Sources from U.S. History, 1877-present

Edited by Jonathan Rees
(Colorado State University—Pueblo)

**For Schlager Group:**
Vice President, Editorial: Sarah Robertson
Vice President, Operations and Strategy: Benjamin Painter
Publisher: Neil Schlager

ISBN: 9781935306719

eISBN: 9781935306467

© 2019 Schlager Group Inc.

All rights reserved. No part of this book may be reproduced or utilized in any form or by any means, electronic or mechanical, including photocopying, recording, or downloading, without permission in writing from the publisher.

For more information,
contact:
1111 W. Mockingbird Lane
STE 735
Dallas, TX 75247
(888-416-5727)
info@MilestoneDocuments.com

Contents

About the Editor — p. 1

Acknowledgments — p. 1

Introduction — p. 2

1.1 The Labor Question — p. 5

    1.2 Edward Atkinson: "The Service Which Capital Renders When Employed by Labor" (1886) — p. 6

    1.3 Wendell Phillips: "The Labor Question" Speech (1872) — p. 9

    1.4 Questions — p. 12

2.1 Native Americans in the American West — p. 13

    2.2 Sarah Winnemucca Hopkins: *Life Among the Piutes* (1883) — p. 14

    2.3 Theodore Roosevelt: *An Autobiography* (1913) — p. 17

    2.4 Questions — p. 20

3.1 Urbanization: The Physical Form and Moral Condition of Cities — p. 21

    3.2 Louis Sullivan: *The Autobiography of an Idea* (1923) — p. 22

    3.3 James W. Buel: *Mysteries and Miseries of America's Great Cities* (1883) — p. 24

    3.4 Questions — p. 27

4.1 The Pure Food and Drug Act — p. 28

4.2 Harvey Wiley: Letter to the Editor of the *Wine Trade Review* (1906) — p. 29

4.3 Hiram Walker & Sons, Ltd.: "A Plot against the People" (1911) — p. 31

4.4 Questions — p. 34

5.1 The Dust Bowl — p. 35

5.2 John Steinbeck: "Starvation under the Orange Trees" (1938) — p. 36

5.3 Frank J. Taylor: "California's Grapes of Wrath" (1939) — p. 39

5.4 Questions — p. 43

6.1 The New Deal and the Role of Government — p. 44

6.2 Franklin D. Roosevelt: Second Inaugural Address (1937) — p. 45

6.3 Charles I. Dawson: "The President Has Made the Issue" (1936) — p. 48

6.4 Questions — p. 50

7.1 Segregation in the North and South — p. 51

7.2 W.E.B. Du Bois: "Segregation in the North" (1934) — p. 52

7.3 Victor H. Green: The Negro Motorist "Green Book" (1940) — p. 54

7.4 Questions — p. 56

8.1 Anti-Communism — p. 57

8.2 Chamber of Commerce of the United States: "Communist Infiltration in the United States: Its Nature and How to Combat It" (1946) — p. 58

8.3 Ryland W. Crary and Gerald L. Steibel: "How You Can Teach About Communism" (1951) — p. 61

8.4 Questions — p. 64

9.1 The Modern Women's Movement — p. 65

9.2 Casey Hayden and Mary King: "Sex and Caste" (1965) — p. 66

9.3 Betty Friedan: Commencement Speech to Smith College Graduates (1981) — p. 68

9.4 Questions — p. 71

10.1 The Generation Gap and the Vietnam War — p. 72

10.2 Lyndon B. Johnson: "Peace without Conquest" Speech about Vietnam (1965) — p. 73

10.3 Raymond Anthony Mungo: Anti-War Speech (1967) — p. 76

10.4 Questions — p. 78

11.1 The Gay Rights Movement — p. 79

11.2 Anita Bryant Is Hit by a Pie (1977) — p. 80

11.3 Harvey Milk: Gay Freedom Day Speech (1978) — p. 82

11.4 Questions — p. 86

12.1 Globalization and the North American Free Trade Agreement — p. 87

12.2 Ross Perot at the Third Presidential Debate (1992) — p. 88

12.3 Bill Clinton: "Remarks on the Signing of NAFTA" (1993) — p. 90

12.4 Questions — p. 93

# About the Editor

Jonathan Rees is Professor of History at Colorado State University—Pueblo. His books include *Refrigeration Nation*, *Before the Refrigerator*, and *Industrialization and the Transformation of American Life*.

# Acknowledgments

**John Steinbeck: "Starvation under the Orange Trees."** "Starvation under the Orange Trees," copyright 1938, renewed 1966 by John Steinbeck; from AMERICA AND AMERICANS AND SELECTED NONFICTION by John Steinbeck, edited by Susan Shillinglaw and Jackson J. Benson. Used by permission of Viking Books, an imprint of Penguin Publishing Group, a division of Penguin Random House LLC. All rights reserved.

**W.E.B. Du Bois: "Segregation in the North."** The publisher wishes to thank the Crisis Publishing Co., Inc., the publisher of the magazine of the National Association for the Advancement of Colored People, for the use of this material first published in the April 1934 issue of *Crisis Magazine*.

# Introduction

Why do you use primary source documents in class? In my case, I'm interested in getting students to understand where historical interpretations originate so that they can make their own. I don't like the God-like detachment of most textbooks, telling everyone exactly what happened without an inch of doubt. Introducing primary sources and explaining their exact relationship to historical events is one way to raise the issues associated with doing history rather than just learning what happened.

Unfortunately, a single document is not always enough to achieve this goal. After all, primary sources have their own shortcomings. The text of a law offers no context. An eyewitness to events can offer only their perspective. Good secondary sources benefit from a wide range of primary sources, so why can't students gain a similar perspective?

That's why I've assembled this collection. The idea is to improve our students' perspectives on particular issues by bringing documents on similar subjects together in order to promote the kinds of analysis that one document alone could never offer.

While three documents can be better than two and four documents can be better than three, the idea behind this collection is to offer enough additional information to improve discussion, but not so much that the additional document provides diminishing returns. While there are always far more than two sides to every story, two documents are enough to hint at a multiplicity of perspectives without bogging a discussion down with so much unnecessary theory that it would confuse anyone in an introductory U.S. History class.

While every document here might not qualify as a milestone in American history, they all suggest issues that any student of American history ought to consider. Of course, the easiest pairs to imagine would be documents from different sides of a single struggle: Republicans versus Democrats, reformers versus the establishment, and so forth. However, not all such contrasts are edifying. Most notably, I didn't want to highlight views that are racist or otherwise wildly out of date. In these instances,

I've leaned towards multiple perspectives on reform or ideas rather than a completely polarized conflict of opinions.

These perspectives are introduced, then followed by discussion questions. The nature of those questions run more along the lines of "Which approach do you think was most successful?" or "How might those approaches have complemented one another?" rather than turning every controversy into a debate about two equivalent sides.

Another thing that document pairs allow teachers to do that can't be done in a single document is hint at the geographical diversity of historical phenomena. "How did segregation in the North compare to segregation in the South?" is one question here, for example.

Since primary sources are what historians use to create their interpretations, how can we as teachers use them to get students to do the same? If one primary source is good for promoting one kind of historical thinking, multiple primary sources can be even better since they suggest even more sophisticated kinds of thought. The more students can make connections between documents to draw conclusions about the past, the more they'll understand what historians do because they'll be doing it themselves in class.

This collection does not include sources dealing with every subject or every time period in American history after 1877. Every teacher makes their own choices about what to cover, and hopefully there will be substantial overlap between what is here and the rest of any particular course where this collection gets used. My criteria for selecting subjects was a combination of historical significance and the ease of demonstrating an important concept with primary source documents.

In my classes, I use documents like these to replace lectures and spark small-group discussion. However, one of the many wonderful things about primary source documents is that they can be adapted for many purposes besides that one. No matter how they are used, what students get by considering these documents together is a glimpse at what historical thinking is about—namely using sources to inspire reasoned analysis based on evidence rather than whatever their textbook happens to tell them.

**Jonathan Rees**
**Colorado State University—Pueblo**

# 1.1 The Labor Question

## Introduction

Industrialization made working harder. New technology made old skills like shoemaking or iron puddling largely obsolete, because in many industries, the factories that relied on new technologies could drastically underprice factories that depended upon skilled labor to produce their wares. This led to enormous instability among working-class Americans who found themselves cast out of once well-paying, stable jobs. Many of those workers formed trade unions to further labor's control of their workplaces, but many of those trade unions were destroyed by anti-union employers and their pro-business allies in government at all levels.

The "Labor Question" was a political argument related to industrialization. While the wording was never standardized, essentially to ask the labor question was to ask how could American workers remain satisfied with their jobs when the circumstances related to industrialization made these jobs increasingly difficult. Ironically, labor itself was never really party to this debate, because most workers would have proposed organizing trade unions, which most Americans with any wealth or power found to be an unacceptable answer. Instead, capital indirectly debated labor sympathizers in the books and magazines of the industrial era about the fate of people who were never party to this extended theoretical conversation.

# 1.2 Edward Atkinson: "The Service Which Capital Renders When Employed by Labor" (1886)

## Document Overview

*Edward Atkinson was an economist and inventor from Brookline, Massachusetts. Although he was an opponent of slavery, the influence of the economist Adam Smith upon him shows here in his justification for capitalist class relations and his dismissal of labor unions. He is a particularly good choice for defending the capitalist side of the Labor Question because he had no direct interest in it. His support was entirely philosophical and is therefore harder to automatically dismiss. Notice too Atkinson's narrow definition of "the right kind of Trades Union."*

## Document Text

...When you justify private property, you admit that capitalists rightly exist. The only question is—if there be any question—at what point the ownership of capital should stop; whether or not it should be forbidden, that, after a man had become possessed of one set of tools, he should be prohibited or prevented from becoming the owner of another set, which he cannot use himself, but which he may let to another man, for a share of the products, who otherwise would be without good tools.

That is all the difference there is between one man and another.

Capital is a tool, an instrument, to be applied to production, to increase the abundance of things. It may be a hammer; it may be a plane; it may be a knitting-needle; it may be a knitting machine; it may be a coined dollar; it may be a hand-loom; it may be a power-loom; it may be a factory or a railroad. These are all alike tools. One man can strike with a hammer which is his tool, who cannot direct the steam-hammer which is another man's tool. The higher you rise in the grade of work from the use of the simple hammer worked by hand to the use of the great trip-hammer worked by the power of steam, the more complex and the more difficult becomes the work, and the more you substitute mental for merely manual skill. You will find, that, in the long run, the tools fall to him who can use them best, provided you do not interfere with the natural order and obstruct the course of events by attempting to stop a great tide which governs all the affairs of men....

There is one thing we all have in common; that is, time. The man who controls his own time and uses it in his own way, is the man who will succeed.

The man who puts the control of his own time into the hands of some other man is pretty sure not to get ahead. The man who combines with others, and who then attempts to control and regulate other men, or to dictate to us what shall be the use of your time and of my time, whether we choose to have him or not, will be pretty sure to get left as soon as the trick is found out. Understand me fully. I do not take the slightest exception to associations of any kind, or to Trades Unions, or to any other organizations or clubs. I belong to a Trades Union myself,—to a Trades Union of the presidents of all the mutual insurance companies that insure the factories in which you work, and keep them from burning up.

We earn our living by saving from destruction by fire the tools by which you get your living. We have combined to put suitable conditions on the owner of every factory to make it safe, and to keep it safe for the protection of life and property.

We cannot force him to adopt them. He controls his own business, and we control ours. Yet he does what we ask him to, to protect the tools with which you earn your living, because he can't afford not to do so.

This is the right kind of a Trades Union.

When you form your associations like the old guilds, and make the condition of membership that every man shall be master of his own art, as well as master of his own time, then you will benefit yourself and everybody else.

Source: Atkinson, Edward. *Addresses upon the Labor Question.* Boston: Franklin Press, 1886.

# 1.3 Wendell Phillips: "The Labor Question" Speech (1872)

## Document Overview

*Wendell Phillips was a prominent abolitionist, woman's rights activist, and advocate for Native Americans. His support for the labor side of the labor question shows that some abolitionists made the connection between the oppression of slaves by masters with the oppression of working-class people by their employers even while other activists like Atkinson didn't. In other words, all these kinds of nineteenth-century activism did not necessarily spring from the exact same set of sympathies.*

## Document Text

Let me tell you why I am interested in the labor question. Not simply because of the long hours of labor; not simply because of a specific oppression of a class. I sympathize with the sufferers there: I am ready to fight on their side. But to look out upon Christendom, with its three hundred millions of people; and I see, that, out of this number of people, one hundred millions never had enough to eat. Physiologists tell us that this body of ours, unless it is properly fed, properly developed, fed with rich blood and carefully nourished, does no justice to the brain. You cannot make a bright or a good man in a starved body; and so this one-third of the inhabitants of Christendom, who have never had food enough, can never be what they should be.

Now, I say that the social civilization which condemns every third man in it to be below the average in the nourishment God prepared for him, did not come from above: it came from below; and, the sooner it goes down, the better. Come on this side of the ocean. You will find forty millions of people, and I suppose they are in the highest state of civilization; and yet it is not too much to say, that, out of that forty millions, ten millions, at least, who get up in the morning and go to bed at night, spend all the day in the mere effort to get bread enough to live. They have not elasticity enough, mind or body, left, to do any thing in the way of intellectual or moral progress.

I take a man, for instance, in one of the manufacturing valleys of Connecticut. If you get into the cars there at 6.30 o'clock in the morning, as I have done, you will find, getting in at every little station, a score or more of laboring men and women, with their dinner in a pail; and they get out at some factory that is already lighted up. Go down the same valley about 7.30 in the evening, and you will again see them going home. They must have got up about 5.30; they are at their work until nigh upon eight o'clock. There is a good, solid fourteen hours. Now, there will be a strong, substantial man, like Cobbett, for instance, who will sit up nights studying, and who will be a scholar at last among them, perhaps; but he is an expert. The average man, nine out of ten, when he gets home at night, does not care to read an article from the "North American," nor a long speech from Charles Sumner. No: if he can't have a good story, and a warm supper, and a glass of grog perhaps, he goes off to bed. Now, I say that the civilization that has produced this state of things in nearly the hundredth year of the American Republic did not come from above.

I believe in the temperance movement. I am a temperance man of nearly forty years' standing; and I think it one of the grandest things in the world, because it holds the basis of self-control. Intemperance is the cause of poverty, I know; but there is another side to that: poverty is the cause of intemperance. Crowd a man with fourteen hours' work a day, and you crowd him down to a mere animal life. You have eclipsed his aspirations, dulled his tastes, stunted his intellect, and made him a mere tool, to work fourteen hours, and catch a thought in the interval; and, while a man in a hundred will rise to be a genius, ninety-nine will cower down under the circumstances. Now, I can tell you a fact. In London, the other day, it was found that one club of gentlemen, a thousand strong, spent twenty thousand dollars at the club-house during the year for drink. Well, I would allow them twenty thousand dollars more at home for liquor, making in all forty thousand dollars a year. These men were all men of education and leisure: they had books and paintings, opera, race-course, and regatta. A thousand men down in Portsmouth in a ship-yard, working under a boss, spent at the grog-shops of the place, in that year, eighty thousand dollars, — double that of their rich brethren. What is the explanation of such a fact as that? Why, the club-man had a circle of pleasures and of company: the operative, after he had worked fourteen hours, had nothing to look forward to but his grog.

That is why I say, lift a man, give him life, let him work eight hours a day, give him the school, develop his taste for music, give him a garden, give him beautiful things to see, and good books to read, and you will starve out those lower appetites. Give a man a chance to earn a good living, and you may save his life.

Source: Phillips, Wendell. *Speeches, Lectures, and Letters.* Boston: Lee and Shepard, 1891.

# 1.4 Questions

1. What qualified either or both of these men to answer the labor question on behalf of others who were directly affected by it?

2. What, if anything, is the relationship between employment and slavery? How is that comparison relevant here?

3. Do workers deserve working conditions and pay that give them the opportunity for leisure as Phillips implies?

# 2.1 Native Americans in the American West

## Introduction

The United States was never empty. From the very beginning of the country's settlement, European immigrants encountered Native American tribes that had lived off the land for centuries. Many of those encounters led to wars that effectively displaced Native Americans from those lands so that Europeans could develop them and exploit whatever natural resources were available. By the late nineteenth century, the trajectory of this struggle had become obvious. The frontier of settlement stretched from the Atlantic to the Pacific, and nothing would stop American settlement from occupying every desirable acre in between.

In 1893 Frederick Jackson Turner famously explained that the frontier had closed, that the American West had effectively been settled by migrants of European ancestry and from elsewhere too. The Native American people who had once had the American West essentially to themselves recognized long before that this would happen and had already begun to adjust their actions accordingly. By 1877 they were massively outnumbered by the new arrivals. While some continued to fight the intruders in whatever ways they had at their disposal, others accepted life on reservations as their fate and experienced life at the mercy of the U.S. government.

# 2.2 Sarah Winnemucca Hopkins: *Life Among the Piutes* (1883)

## Document Overview

*The Northern Paiute tribe once controlled what is now northern Nevada and eastern California. Sarah Winnemucca Hopkins, a chief's daughter, was an activist who wanted both to draw attention to the plight of her people and to tell the story of white/Native American relations from the perspective of the Native Americans. This excerpt from her book* Life Among the Piutes *[sic] is a long quote from a chief named Egan describing the broken promises that the Northern Paiute faced on reservations in 1878.*

## Document Text

When our good father, Sam Parrish, was here, oh, then we were happy. Our children were not crying for anything to eat, and causing our hearts to ache for them. We all had everything we wanted, we had plenty of clothes, and were all doing well. And you, our dear mother, told us the truth. You told us that Sam was going away, and that there was a Christian agent to be sent here in his place; but you said you knew he would not do for us like our father Parrish. Oh, it was too true! Here we are all starving under this Christian man. He has not made any issues of clothing since he came here. After he discharged you, and you were gone, he called for a council, and all went to hear what he had to say. He told us that if we did not like the way he did, all we had to do was to leave the place, that he did not care, and he also said, "If my interpreter does not do as I want him to, he can go too. The government is not going to fool with you. Now if you want to work, the government will pay you one dollar a day." I, chief of the Snake River Piutes, stopped the agent by saying, "I want to talk a little." I commenced by saying, "You are a good man. You talk with our Great Father up in the Spirit-land. You look up to the sky, and make us think you are a good Christian, and we want you to tell us the truth, not lies. We know nothing. We don't read, and therefore we don't know what to think. You, who are greater than anybody, say that this is government land, not land for us; and you say we must work for government, and government will pay us one dollar a day for our work. Yes, we will work for the government for money, for we love money just as well as you do,—you good Christian men who have come here. We were told by our good agent, Sam Parrish, that this land was ours for all to work upon and make us homes here. He also told us the government had set it apart for us Indians, and government would help us all if we would help ourselves, and that we must always be ready to go to work at whatever work he put us to, and that everything we raised on the place was ours, and the annuities that were sent here were given to us by our good father Parrish. He gave us everything our hearts could wish for. He also told me to tell all my people who had no homes to come here and go to work like white men. The white folk have to work very hard and we must do the same. Our good agent never had any trouble with us, because we would do everything we could to please him, and he did the same by us. He gave us our annuities without saying 'You must do this or that, or you leave here.' No: he treated us as if were his children, and we returned his kindness by doing everything he set us to do. He was with us two years, and we were all happy. He did not shoot our ponies because the ponies broke the fences, but he would say, 'Your horses have broken into your grain, look out for them'; and then we would run and get them out and mend the fences. He did not do like you, good Christian man, by saying, 'Here, my men, go and shoot those Indians' horses! They are in our grain.' Our father Parrish told us all to be good and never take any stray horses that came on our agency; nor did he want us to go and get stray horses. Have you done so? No: you and your men have done everything that is bad. You have taken up every horse that came along here, and you have them in your stable, and you are working them. And another thing, your men are doing what Parrish told us not to do, that is gambling. You and your men have brought a book amongst us that has big chiefs' pictures and their wives' pictures on the papers, and another picture which you call Jack, and another something like it.

And with these your men come to our camps, and gamble with your interpreter and your mail-carrier, every time you pay them off. This is what your blacksmith Johnson is doing; and your school-teacher, Frank Johnson, instead of teaching my people's children, does more gambling than teaching. What you pay to your interpreter and mail-carrier, the two Johnsons win back again with the book that you brought here. So we are at a loss to know which of you are right: whether Sam Parrish told us lies or you, or our chieftain's daughter, Sarah Winnemucca, about the land being ours; and you who talk with our Great Father in the Spirit-land three times a day, have come here and told us the land is not ours.' This is what I said to the agent after you left us, and now you have come and found me almost starved.

Now one and all of you, my men, give our mother what little money you have. Let her go and talk for us. Let her go right on to Washington, and have a talk with our Great Father in Washington.

Source: Hopkins, Sarah Winnemucca. *Life Among the Piutes: Their Wrongs and Claims.* Edited by Horace Mann. Boston: Cupples, Upham & Co, 1883.

# 2.3 Theodore Roosevelt: *An Autobiography* (1913)

## Document Overview

*Theodore Roosevelt was a naturalist, historian and, of course, politician. After his presidency ended in 1913, he wrote an autobiography that, in part, looked back on his brief career as a rancher in what is now North Dakota during the mid-1880s. Here he examines the relationship between local settlers and the Native Americans who remained in that area.*

## Document Text

When I went West, the last great Indian wars had just come to an end, but there were still sporadic outbreaks here and there, and occasionally bands of marauding young braves were a menace to outlying and lonely settlements. Many of the white men were themselves lawless and brutal, and prone to commit outrages on the Indians. Unfortunately, each race tended to hold all the members of the other race responsible for the misdeeds of a few, so that the crime of the miscreant, red or white, who committed the original outrage too often invited retaliation upon entirely innocent people, and this action would in its turn arouse bitter feeling which found vent in still more indiscriminate retaliation. The first year I was on the Little Missouri some Sioux bucks ran off all the horses of a buffalo-hunter's outfit. One of the buffalo-hunters tried to get even by stealing the horses of a Cheyenne hunting party, and when pursued made for a cow camp, with, as a result, a longrange skirmish between the cowboys and the Cheyennes. One of the latter was wounded; but this particular wounded man seemed to have more sense than the other participants in the chain of wrong-doing, and discriminated among the whites. He came into our camp and had his wound dressed.

A year later I was at a desolate little mud road ranch on the Deadwood trail. It was kept by a very capable and very forceful woman, with sound ideas of justice and abundantly well able to hold her own. Her husband was a worthless devil, who finally got drunk on some whisky he obtained from an outfit of Missouri bull-whackers—that is, freighters, driving ox wagons. Under the stimulus of the whisky he picked a quarrel with his wife and attempted to beat her. She knocked him down with a stove-lid lifter, and the admiring bull-whackers bore him off, leaving the lady in full possession of the ranch. When I visited her she had a man named Crow Joe working for her, a slab-sided, shifty-eyed person who later, as I heard my foreman explain, "skipped the country with a bunch of horses." The mistress of the ranch made first-class buckskin shirts of great durability. The one she made for me, and which I used for years, was used by one of my sons in Arizona a couple of winters ago. I had ridden down into the country after some lost horses, and visited the ranch to get her to make me the buckskin shirt in question. There were, at the moment, three Indians there, Sioux, well behaved and self-respecting, and she explained to me that they had been resting there waiting for dinner, and that a white man had come along and tried to run off their horses. The Indians were on the lookout, however, and, running out, they caught the man; but, after retaking their horses and depriving him of his gun, they let him go. "I don't see why they let him go," exclaimed my hostess. "I don't believe in stealing Indians' horses any more than white folks'; so I told 'em they could go along and hang him—I'd never cheep. Anyhow, I won't charge them anything for their dinner," concluded my hostess. She was in advance of the usual morality of the time and place, which drew a sharp line between stealing citizens' horses and stealing horses from the Government or the Indians.

A fairly decent citizen, Jap Hunt, who long ago met a violent death, exemplified this attitude towards Indians in some remarks I once heard him make. He had started a horse ranch, and had quite honestly purchased a number of broken-down horses of different brands, with the view of doctoring them and selling them again. About this time there had been much horse-stealing and cattle-killing in our Territory and in Montana, and under the direction of some of the big cattle-growers a committee of vigilantes had been organized to take action against the rustlers, as the horse thieves and cattle thieves were called. The vigilantes, or stranglers, as they were locally known, did their work thoroughly; but, as always happens with bodies of the kind, toward the end they grew reckless in their actions, paid off private grudges, and hung men on slight provocation. Riding into Jap Hunt's ranch, they nearly hung him because he had so many horses of different brands. He was finally let off. He was much upset by the incident, and explained again and again, "The idea of saying that I was a horse thief! Why, I never stole a horse in my life—leastways from a white man. I don't count Indians nor the Government, of course." Jap had been reared among men still in the stage of tribal morality, and while they recognized their obligations to one another, both the Government and the Indians seemed alien bodies, in regard to which the laws of morality did not apply.

On the other hand, parties of savage young bucks would treat lonely settlers just as badly, and in addition sometimes murder them. Such a party was generally composed of young fellows burning to distinguish themselves. Some one of their number would have obtained a pass from the Indian Agent allowing him to travel off the reservation, which pass would be flourished whenever their action was questioned by bodies of whites of equal strength.

Source: Roosevelt, Theodore. *An Autobiography*. New York: Charles Scribner's Sons, 1913.

## 2.4 Questions

1. Why might Native Americans have resisted the move to reservations despite the overwhelming force that the American government used against them?

2. Compare and contrast the attitude of Native Americans and whites towards the natural resources of the West as reflected in these documents.

3. How does this passage from Roosevelt's autobiography reflect his attitudes towards various groups in the West, including Native Americans, cowboys, and even the Japanese?

# 3.1 Urbanization: The Physical Form and Moral Condition of Cities

## Introduction

In the late nineteenth and early twentieth centuries, cities grew rapidly. Cities were the sites of new factories. Those factories attracted immigrants, who moved to cities because that's where the jobs were. There was also a huge internal migration from rural areas. As farming became increasingly automated, it became harder for children (both male and female) to stay on the farm and have a stable, prosperous life. As a result, there was a popular anti-urban movement, which played up the risks to the physical and moral health of those moving to cities.

The physical structure of cities grew both outward and upward. The number of people who could move to the newly emerging suburbs were limited by the ability of suburbanites to transport themselves into the city for work and return to suburbia each day. Streetcar lines, and later automobiles, increasingly made moving further away a feasible option. The number of people who could work in urban areas was limited by the number of offices, and later apartments for people to live closer to their places of employment. Building skyscrapers made it possible to fit more people in these limited areas. Yet even before skyscrapers became common in American cities, an anti-urban movement arose to point out to potential city-dwellers all the problems that came when lots of people lived so close together.

# 3.2 Louis Sullivan: *The Autobiography of an Idea* (1923)

## Document Overview

*Louis Sullivan was the first—and after his one-time protege Frank Lloyd Wright—the best-known of what came to be known as the Chicago School of architects. Sullivan did not invent the idea of the skyscraper, but nonetheless he pioneered its development. As this excerpt from his book* The Autobiography of an Idea *shows, Sullivan was just as concerned about how tall buildings looked as he was about how much money they could make for their owners, who rented out space in them. Sullivan clearly relished the challenge of constructing beautiful tall buildings in his native city of Chicago, but he also recognized that failing this challenge had the potential to create social problems.*

## Document Text

It was inherent in the nature of masonry construction, in its turn to fix a new limit to height, as its ever thickening walls ate up ground and floor space of ever increasing value, as the pressure of population rapidly increased....

Thus arose a crisis, a seeming *impasse*. What was to do? Architects made attempts at solutions by carrying the outer spans of floor loads on cast columns next to the masonry piers, but this method was of small avail, and of limited application as to height. The attempts, moreover, did not rest on any basic principle, therefore the squabbling as to priority are so much piffle. The problem of the tall office building had not been solved, because the solution had not been sought within the problem itself—within its inherent nature....

The need was there, the capacity to satisfy was there, but contact was not there. Then came the flash of imagination which saw the single thing. The trick was turned; and there swiftly came into being something new under the sun. For the true steel-frame structure stands unique in the flowing of man and his works; a brilliant material example of man's capacity to satisfy his needs through the exercise of his natural powers. The tall steel-frame structure may have its aspects of beneficence; but so long as a man may say: "I shall do as I please with my own," it presents opposite aspects of social menace and danger. For such is the complexity, the complication, the intricacy of modern feudal society; such is its neurasthenia, its hyperesthesia, its precarious instability, that not a move may be in one of its manifold activities, according to its code, without creating risk and danger in its wake....

The architects of Chicago welcome the steel frame and did something with it. The architects of the East were appalled by it and could make no contribution to it. In fact, the tall office buildings fronting the narrow streets and lanes of lower New York were provincialisms, gross departures from the law of common sense. For the tall office building loses its validity when the surroundings are uncongenial to its nature; and when such buildings are crowded together upon narrow streets or lanes they become mutually destructive.... The appeal and the inspiration lie, of course, in the element of loftiness, in the suggestion of slenderness and aspiration, the soaring quality as of a thing rising from the earth as a unitary utterance, Dionysian in beauty. The failure to observe this simple truth has resulted in a throng of monstrosities, snobbish and maudlin or brassy insolent or thick-lipped in speech;
in either case a defamation and denial of man's finest powers.

Source: Sullivan, Louis. "The Autobiography of an Idea." *The Journal of the American Institute of Architects* 6, no. 1 (January 1923): 337-38.

# 3.3 James W. Buel: *Mysteries and Miseries of America's Great Cities* (1883)

## Document Overview

*There was not one but two waves of movement to America's cities during the late-nineteenth and early twentieth centuries. Immigrants came from overseas and often moved directly to cities where they might find others from their homeland already residing. The other wave was from America's rural areas. With land less available and mechanization making farming far less appealing than it had once been, many young people moved to the cities for both economic and cultural reasons. Buel's book is typical of many works from this period designed to both scare and entice potential urbanites. While fear of crowds has always been a low-grade fright for nearly everyone who is not familiar with urban life, the idea that cities proved an acute moral threat to women of all kinds reflects the unique puritanical anxieties of Victorian-era America.*

## Document Text

The first visit to New York is always productive of a singular sensation—a realization of your utter inconsequence in the world; a feeling that every one who swells the crowd and rush of Broadway is of infinitely of more importance than yourself, and that you are as much out of your sphere as though some mighty occult force had suddenly transported you to a strange planet, the inhabitants of which were rushing wildly about in their efforts to destroy themselves and every world in the infinite firmament. In such a mass of princes and beggars, natives and strangers, the visitor is kept dodging, halting and shuffling to avoid the pressing throng, which, though utterly unobserving, he believes are tickling themselves at his unsophisticated and ludicrous actions. The confusing rattle of busses and wagons over the granite pavement in Broadway almost drowns his own thoughts, and if he should desire to cross the street a thousand misgivings will assail him, for although he sees scores of men and women constantly passing through the moving lines of vehicles, it gives him little courage to attempt it himself, because his confidence has deserted him the moment he leaves the car that has brought him to the city. It happens, therefore, not infrequently that a stranger will suffer the pressure of a hurrying and jostling crowd on the sidewalk for an hour before plucking up sufficient resolution to attempt a crossing, and even when the effort is made he feels like shutting his eyes to hide from sight the result. If the visitor should chance to be the custodian of large funds, he clutches the wallet that contains them with many doubts of his ability to prevent their disappearance; he looks on every strange face with suspicion, which feeling he never exchanges for confidence until some one speaks familiarly to him, when his anxiety for companionship very frequently leads him to adopt a stranger for a friend, and makes him susceptible to the sharp practices of designing villains. To this very cause is due the fact that so many visitors are robbed, for though a man may be a resident of another large city, and familiar with the cunning ways of confidence men, being a stranger in New York he loses his composure and becomes often a ready victim through a desire to make acquaintance with some one, without requiring or considering antecedents.

What is true of men, with respect to their gullibility, is also true of women, only the latter are generally more easily beguiled for reasons apparent enough. Thousands of women visit New York every month in the year without escorts or any knowledge of the city; many of them are prompted solely by curiosity,—perhaps the love of adventure and to establish some agreeable acquaintance; others conceive the idea that so large a city furnishes abundant means for innocent enjoyment, and that wealthy wife-seekers are as plentiful there as blackberries in harvest time. Some go to New York to gratify a longing ambition; some in search of missing friends, and thousands of beautiful but unfortunate young girls go there hoping to find honorable situations to support themselves, and perhaps sick and destitute parents. Heaven show pity for the latter!

The pretty woman who visits New York without a friend to counsel her, and without any knowledge of the city, is like one caught trenching upon the grounds of Giant Slay-Good. She may be full of resolution, and coronated with the jewels of chastity, yet the psychologizing influence of oppressive lonesomeness, the wiles of da-do young libertines, or, lastly, the seductive representations of gaudily robed and matronly appearing procuresses, will surely destroy her wholesome decisions and turn her into the path that leads away from God.

But with all the snares laid for the feet of young girls and beautiful women visiting New York, they are not half so successful in entrapping victims as is the influence of gold in accomplishing the spoliation of attractive women who are residents of the Metropolis. The almighty power of riches is a veritable harvester of virtue, while following close behind wealth is the deferential and persuasive gleaner who accomplishes his purposes by either effrontery, promises of marriage, his good looks, or sugar-coated protestations and love syllables. After the reapers and gleaners have passed through the fruiting time of chastity, only wilted straws and stray buds remain.

Source: Buell, James W. *Mysteries and Miseries of America's Great Cities: Embracing New York, Washington City, San Francisco, Salt Lake City, and New Orleans.* St. Louis: Historical Publishing Co., 1883.

# 3.4 Questions

1. How does Sullivan make the case for cities through explaining the origins of skyscrapers? Would most people have felt the need to make that case at all? Why or why not?

2. Which audience do you think Buel's text was aimed at? How can you tell from the text itself?

3. How could Americans have weighed the advantages and disadvantages of living in the cities?

# 4.1 The Pure Food and Drug Act

## Introduction

The Progressive Era lasted roughly from the 1890s to 1914. During that time, many laws passed Congress and state legislatures that were designed to reform society for the better. Progressive reformers often debated priorities over which laws to enact first. However, they tended to favor the same general principles such as efficient government, increased regulation, and promoting public safety. While these laws sound good in principle to modern ears, it is harder to understand what those laws actually did because of the way they were enforced.

A case in point is the Pure Food Law, now known as the Pure Food and Drug Act of 1906 (PFDA), the first major piece of progressive legislation passed at the federal level. On the one hand, Dr. Harvey Wiley—head of the Bureau of Chemistry at the U.S. Department of Agriculture, the agency first charged with enforcing that law—tried to get it enforced in as broad a way possible. On the other hand, many food manufacturers objected that Wiley's interpretations of the law violated the intent of Congress when they passed it. These manufacturers were not anti-regulation, but they did not believe that the strictest regulation possible would be good for business or consumers.

# 4.2 Harvey Wiley: Letter to the Editor of the *Wine Trade Review* (1906)

## Document Overview

*Wiley was one of the major forces behind the passage of the PFDA in 1906. As part of that law, his bureau and Wiley himself played a major role in enforcing it. However, Wiley's Bureau of Chemistry was charged merely with determining whether a particular food had been adulterated with substances that could do consumers harm or somehow deceived them, not with what the government should do to prevent violations. Even before the passage of the PFDA, Wiley expressed his hostility towards any kind of whiskey that was not aged in oak barrels calling itself whiskey. In this letter, he explains why only particularly made alcoholic beverages should be allowed to use particular names.*

## Document Text

By the word "purity," as applied to distilled spirits and beverages, I mean that they are true to name and are exactly what they are represented to be or what the consumer believes them to be. As an illustration, I may say that the word "brandy," as I understand it, should be applied solely to the product obtained by the distillation of sound wine. This product is placed in wood and kept in storage a sufficient time to allow the ripening process to fully develop. Alcohol which comes from any other source than from the distillation of wine is not admitted into a substance known and sold as brandy.

In like manner "purity" as applied to whisky, as I understand it, means a product obtained by the fermentation of cereals, the starch of which has been converted into sugar by the action of malt. This distillate is collected and stored, as in the case of brandy. The distillate in each case should contain the whole of the volatile matters, whatever be their nature, which are converted during fermentation, except possibly some of those which come over at the very first or at the very last of the distillation. In other words, the still must not be a chambered still, though it may separate some of the more objectionable products in the usual method of preparation.

While I should have no objection to the manufacture of compounded beverages nor to their sale and consumption, provided no deleterious substance is used in their production, I think they should be sold under distinct names, so as to clearly indicate to the consumer that they are compounds. I certainly should have no objection to the manufacture and sale of a blended whisky, meaning by a blended whisky one which is made from mixtures of two or more whiskies. If these mixtures are of different ages, the age of the oldest one should not be used in connection with the label.

Scotch whisky, from the best evidence which I can collect, was originally made by the fermentation of barley malt without the addition of other cereals, and the whisky was made and its reputation established in accordance with this method of manufacture. In this case Scotch whisky is a name which should be applied only to the product obtained by the distillation of the fermented mash of barley malt. More over, this distillation should be carried on in a pot still, as described above, and the product stored in wood and suitably aged. If I have been correctly informed, the so-called "smoky flavor" of Scotch whisky is due to the fact that malt, after sprouting, is dried over burning peat, which imparts the empyreumatic flavor thereof. If this be the case, the addition of a substance known as "essence of Scotch whisky" to any other kind or kinds of alcohol or to any other whisky or mixture could not possibly convert such a product into Scotch whisky. Further than this, the admixture of greater or less quantities of high wines or pure alcohol with genuine Scotch whisky could not make a mixture which should be called by the name of Scotch whisky.

Source: House of Representatives, United States. *Hearings before the Committee on Agriculture.* Washington, DC: Government Printing Office, 1906.

# 4.3 Hiram Walker & Sons, Ltd.: "A Plot against the People" (1911)

## Document Overview

*Hiram Walker & Sons is a Canadian distiller founded by an American, Hiram Walker, in 1858. The company's whiskey was created by a method that did not fit with Harvey Wiley's conception of what whiskey was. Therefore, it lobbied heavily against Wiley's interpretation of the PFDA as it applied to whiskey and attacked Wiley personally because of this issue. This section of "A Plot against the People" takes a legalistic angle rather than the personal attacks found in much of the rest of the pamphlet. President William Howard Taft favored Walker's position on what could be called whiskey in a 1909 executive order. Nevertheless, this pamphlet went through multiple editions (including this one issued in 1911) because Wiley remained a controversial figure.*

## Document Text

### The Pure Food Law—Its Objects and Requirements

> Its objects are: "To preserve the health of the people"; to "prevent their being deceived by label or brand."— (President Taft). "The primary purpose is to protect against fraud."
> — (Attorney General Bonaparte).

> It does not say that articles *must be* branded or labelled in some way, but only that they must *not* be *falsely* branded or labelled.

> It does not say to what extent brands or labels shall be descriptive: consequently, if any one of the many kinds of Cheese is branded simply CHEESE, the law is satisfied.

> It neither establishes nor refers to any FOOD STANDARDS.

President Taft says: "It does not authorize any officers to fix a STANDARD in respect to *any* article of food."

It gives no officials, (chemists or others), power to *decide* what is illegal. It provides that when chemists *consider* an article to be adulterated or misbranded, the party interested shall be entitled to a hearing by the Secretary of Agriculture. If, after that, the article is *still* considered to be adulterated or misbranded, the proper District Attorney shall take action *in the Courts* to determine the question.

As the means of bringing the article before the courts, a "seizure" of it is to be made. It is obvious that a *single* "seizure" of the same article, and of a *single* package of it, is sufficient; as it would be absurd to suppose that Congress intended there should be *numerous* suits in *numerous* courts at the *one* time on the *one* question.

It does not suggest the changing of old names. It is obvious that to deceive the public by the improper use of a name, it must be a name which they *already know*. The Law embraces Liquors under the head of FOODS.

The Act does not once mention WHISKY. Its provisions apply generally, and to one food equally with any other. Therefore, it requires in regard to WHISKY no more and no less than in regard to BUTTER, or SUGAR, or COFFEE, or TEA.

The interpretation of the Act is a matter for Lawyers. A judge always *instructs* a jury as to what the law is: they never decide *that*.

The proper name for any Food is a question of fact, to be decided by evidence. A Judge always leaves the Jury to decide what the facts are. The question is—"What article and what name go together in the minds of the public?"

Source: Robbins, William, ed. *A Plot against the People: A History of the Audacious Attempt by Certain Kentucky "Straight Whisky"*

*Interests to Pervert the Pure Food Law in Order to Create a Monopoly for Their Fusel Oil Whiskies and to Outlaw All Refined Whiskies.* Wakerville, Ontario, Canada: Hiram Walker & Sons, Ltd., 1911.

## 4.4 Questions

1. Why is Wiley so concerned about how whiskey is marketed, since it's not as if drinking the pure stuff makes it any healthier?

2. Which of these documents reveals a better understanding of the spirit of the Pure Food and Drug Act? Why?

3. Should the way that a law is enforced strictly confirm to the letter of that law, even if the new manner in which it is enforced benefits society as a whole? Why or why not?

# 5.1 The Dust Bowl

## Introduction

The Dust Bowl refers to the worst drought in American history. It struck areas of Oklahoma, Texas, Kansas, Colorado, and New Mexico from approximately 1932 to 1940. While this area had undergone frequent droughts to this point in time, what made this one so bad was the over-farming of marginal areas during the boom times during and following World War I. Grasses that had once kept the soil from flying when rain was sparse had been plowed under for wheat. Thus, they were no longer there when drought returned to the region. The result was a devastating environmental and human catastrophe, as massive dust storms enveloped the region. As their farmland disappeared and with the country in the midst of the Great Depression, farm families left the region in large numbers, seeking a better life elsewhere.

The resulting migration made this weather event doubly important, as it affected two different regions of the country. Many of the people who had grown wheat in the Dust Bowl packed up all their belongings and moved to California to pick fruit and other crops, in response to growers there soliciting the migrants' services in the hopes of lowering their labor costs. The conditions the migrants faced in California were frequently difficult.

# 5.2 John Steinbeck: "Starvation under the Orange Trees" (1938)

## Document Overview

*The experience of these farmers and their families was immortalized in the 1939 novel* The Grapes of Wrath, *by California writer John Steinbeck. Few people recognize that Steinbeck's work was based upon on-the-scene reporting. Here is part of one of the stories Steinbeck wrote for the* Monterey Trader *(his local paper).*

## Document Text

There has been no war in California, no plague, no bombing of open towns and roads, no shelling of cities. It is a beautiful year. And thousands of families are starving in California. In the county seats the coroners are filling in "malnutrition" in the spaces left for "causes of death." For some reason, a coroner shrinks from writing "starvation" when a thin child is dead in a tent.

For it's in the tents you see along the roads and in the shacks built from dump heap material that the hunger is, and it isn't malnutrition. It is starvation. Malnutrition means you go without certain food essentials and take a long time to die, but starvation means no food at all. The green grass spreads right into the tent doorways and the orange trees are loaded. In the cotton fields, a few wisps of the old crop cling to the black stems. But the people who picked the cotton, and cut the peaches and apricots, who crawled all day in the rows of lettuce and beans, are hungry. The men who harvested the crops of California, the women and girls who stood all day and half the night in the canneries, are starving.

It was so two years ago in Nipomo, it is so now, it will continue to be so until the rich produce of California can be grown and harvested on some other basis than that of stupidity and greed. What is to be done about it? The Federal Government is trying to feed and give direct relief, but it is difficult to do quickly for there are forms to fill out, questions to ask, for fear someone who isn't actually starving may get something. The state relief organizations are trying to send those who haven't been in the state for a year back to the states they came from. The Associated Farmers, which presumes to speak for the farms of California and which is made up of such earth-stained toilers as chain banks, public utilities, railroad companies and those huge corporations called land companies, this financial organization in the face of the crisis is conducting Americanism meetings and bawling about reds and foreign agitators. It has been invariably true in the past that when such a close-knit financial group as the Associated Farmers becomes excited about our ancient liberties and foreign agitators, someone is about to lose something.

A wage cut has invariably followed such a campaign of pure Americanism. And of course any resentment of such a wage cut is set down as the work of foreign agitators. Anyway that is the Associated Farmers contribution to the hunger of the men and women who harvest their crops. The small farmers, who do not belong to the Associated Farmers and cannot make use of the slop chest, are helpless to do anything about it. The little storekeepers at crossroads and in small towns have carried the accounts of the working people until they are near to bankruptcy....

It may be of interest to reiterate the reasons why these people are in the state and the reason they must go hungry. They are here because we need them. Before the white American migrants were here, it was the custom in California to import great numbers of Mexicans, Filipinos, Japanese, to keep them segregated, to herd them about like animals, and, if there were any complaints, to deport or to imprison the leaders. This system of labor was a dream of heaven to such employers as those who now fear foreign agitators so much.

But then the dust and the tractors began displacing the sharecroppers of Oklahoma, Texas, Kansas and Arkansas. Families who had lived for many years on the little "cropper lands" were dispossessed because the land was in the hands of the banks and finance companies, and because these owners found that one man with a tractor could do the work of ten sharecropper families.

Faced with the question of starving or moving, these dispossessed families came west. To a certain extent they were actuated by advertisements and handbills distributed by labor contractors from California. It is to the advantage of the corporate farmer to have too much labor, for then wages can be cut. Then people who are hungry will fight each other for a job rather than the employer for a living wage.

It is possible to make money for food and gasoline for at least nine months of the year if you are quick on the getaway, if your wife and children work in the fields. But then the dead three months strikes, and what can you do then? The migrant cannot save anything. It takes everything he can make to feed his family and buy gasoline to go to the next job. If you don't believe this, go out in the cotton fields next year. Work all day and see if you have made thirty-five cents. A good picker makes more, of course, but you can't.

Source: Steinbeck, John. "Starvation under the Orange Trees." In *America and Americans and Selected Nonfiction,* edited by Susan Shillinglaw and Jackson J. Benson. New York: Penguin, 2002.

# 5.3 Frank J. Taylor: "California's Grapes of Wrath" (1939)

## Document Overview

*After the publication of Steinbeck's novel, California growers did their best to contradict his depiction of conditions on their farms. Read just a little of this essay from the Associated Farmers of Fresno County, Inc., and it becomes apparent that they and Steinbeck had very different conceptions of how the American free enterprise system ought to work.*

## Document Text

### NO JOADS HERE

The Joad family of nine, created by Steinbeck to typify the "Okie" migrants, is anything but typical. A survey made for the Farm Security Administration revealed that thirty was the average age of migrant adults, that the average family had 2.8 children.

Steinbeck's Joads, once arrived in the "land of promise," earned so little that they faced slow starvation. Actually, no migrant family hungers in California unless it is too proud to accept relief. Few migrants are.

There is no red tape about getting free food or shelter.

The FSA maintains warehouses in eleven strategically located towns, where the grant officer is authorized to issue 15 days' rations to any migrant who applies, identifies himself by showing his driver's license, and answers a few simple questions about his family, his earnings, and his travels. In emergencies, the grant officer may issue money for clothing, gasoline, or medical supplies. The food includes standard brands of a score of staple products, flour, beans, corn meal, canned milk and tomatoes, dried fruit, and other grocery items. Before the 15 days are up, the grant officer or his assistant visits the migrant family in camp, and, if the need still exists, the ration is renewed repeatedly until the family finds work.

Shelter is provided by the FSA (a unit of the Federal Resettlement Administration) at model camps which Steinbeck himself represents as satisfactory. The one at Shafter is typical. A migrant family is assigned to a wooden platform on which a tent may be pitched; if the family lacks a tent, the camp has some to lend. The rent is a dime a day, and the migrant who wants to save the money can work it out by helping to clean up camp. The dime goes into a community benefit fund, administered by a committee. Camp facilities include toilets, showers and laundry tubs, with hot and cold running water, a community house. These thirteen camps cost around $190,000 apiece, and each accommodates some three hundred families. Last summer there were vacant platforms, though in winter there is a shortage of space.

Various relief organizations divide the responsibility of providing food and shelter for California's migrants. Federal authorities, working through the FSA, assume the burden for the first year. After a migrant family has been in the State a year, it becomes eligible for State relief. After three years, it becomes a county charge. State relief for agricultural workers averages $51 a month in California, as compared with $21 in Oklahoma, less for several neighboring States. The U. S. Farm Placement Service notes that WPA wages in California are $44 per month, in Oklahoma $32. California old-age pensions are $32 per month, Oklahoma's $20. These are U. S. Social Security Board figures. Records of the FSA grant offices indicate that many migrants earned under $200 a year back home—or less than one third the relief allowance in California. Thus thousands of Okies, having discovered this comparative bonanza, urge their kinsfolk to join them in California, where the average migrant family earns $400 during the harvest season and is able, after the first lean year, to draw an equal sum for relief during eight months of enforced idleness....

# STUBBORN INDIVIDUALISTS

An inference of *The Grapes of Wrath* is that most of the California farmlands are in great holdings, operated by corporations or land "barons." The State has 6,732,390 acres devoted to crops, and the 1935 census shows that 1,738,906 are in farms less than 100 acres in extent, 3,068,742 are in farms of 100 to 1,000 acres, and 1,924,742 are in farms of over 1,000. An insinuation of *The Grapes of Wrath* is that wages are forced down by the Associated Farmers and the Bank of America, acting in conspiracy. Actually, neither the Association nor the Bank concerns itself with wages. Rates of pay are worked out through the farmer co-operatives in each crop or through local groups, such as the San Joaquin Regional Council, which agrees each spring on a base wage. California farmers pay higher wages than those of any State but Connecticut, according to the U. S. Farm Placement Bureau.

This same federal organization conducted an inquiry into the charge, aired in *The Grapes of Wrath,* that California farmers had distributed handbills through the dust-bowl area, offering jobs to lure a surplus of migrant labor to the State. Only two cases were unearthed, one by a labor contractor in Santa Barbara County, another by an Imperial Valley contractor. The licenses of both have since been revoked. At the Associated Farmers head office in San Francisco, I saw hundreds of clippings from Midwest newspapers—publicity inspired by the Association-advising migrants not to
come to California.

The problem of connecting migrant workers who want jobs with farmers who need help is serious. A rumor will sweep like wildfire through migrant camps, of jobs in some valley hundreds of miles distant. Two days later that valley is swamped with so many workers that the harvest which ordinarily would last a month is finished in a week. The U. S. Department of Labor, working with the State Employment Office, now maintains job-information services in eighty-one towns and cities. At any of these offices, migrant workers may check on job prospects in any other area. But most workers still prefer to take a chance.

Source: Taylor, Frank J. *California's Grapes of Wrath*. Associated Farmers of Fresno County, Inc., 1939.

# 5.4 Questions

1. Do Steinbeck and Taylor differ about the cause of the Dust Bowl migration or just over what should be done about it?

2. Do Steinbeck and Taylor agree on anything? If so, what?

3. What were the responsibilities of growers to the migrants who picked their crops? Did they meet them?

# 6.1 The New Deal and the Role of Government

## Introduction

When the stock market crashed in 1929, the economy did not crash overnight. Instead there was a slow slide to the bottom that overwhelmed President Herbert Hoover's 1932 re-election bid—and likely would have done the same to any other politician running on the Republican ticket. The Democratic candidate, Franklin D. Roosevelt, introduced the term *New Deal* during that campaign, but he offered little detail about which laws he would recommend or programs he would create as part of this effort when he became president. During the first hundred days of his presidency, a compliant Congress passed a whole slew of efforts aimed at promoting relief, reform, and economic recovery during a years-long crisis that would become known as the Great Depression.

While many of the laws that implemented these programs were struck down as unconstitutional during Roosevelt's first term, many others persisted. Some, like the Social Security Act, remain in place today. For this reason, the New Deal is important not just for its effects on America during the 1930s; it also marks a change among Americans in how they viewed government in general. Since the New Deal, many Americans have looked to the government for help during dark times. Much of the modern political debate involves how much help the government should provide.

# 6.2 Franklin D. Roosevelt: Second Inaugural Address (1937)

## Document Overview

*When Franklin D. Roosevelt took the oath of office as president for the second time in 1937, most of his New Deal program to combat the Great Depression had already passed through Congress and had started to be implemented. While the programs had varying degrees of success and popularity, Roosevelt felt the need to justify what he did during this speech in the hope of getting more legislation passed. The fact that his second term saw the addition of relatively few additional laws shows that the sense of urgency that existed at the start of his first term was beginning to dissipate.*

## Document Text

My fellow countrymen. When four years ago we met to inaugurate a President, the Republic, single-minded in anxiety, stood in spirit here. We dedicated ourselves to the fulfillment of a vision—to speed the time when there would be for all the people that security and peace essential to the pursuit of happiness. We of the Republic pledged ourselves to drive from the temple of our ancient faith those who had profaned it; to end by action, tireless and unafraid, the stagnation and despair of that day. We did those first things first.

Our covenant with ourselves did not stop there. Instinctively we recognized a deeper need—the need to find through government the instrument of our united purpose to solve for the individual the ever-rising problems of a complex civilization. Repeated attempts at their solution without the aid of government had left us baffled and bewildered. For, without that aid, we had been unable to create those moral controls over the services of science which are necessary to make science a useful servant instead of a ruthless master of mankind. To do this we knew that we must find practical controls over blind economic forces and blindly selfish men.

We of the Republic sensed the truth that democratic government has innate capacity to protect its people against disasters once considered inevitable, to solve problems once considered unsolvable. We would not admit that we could not find a way to master economic epidemics just as, after centuries of fatalistic suffering, we had found a way to master epidemics of disease. We refused to leave the problems of our common welfare to be solved by the winds of chance and the hurricanes of disaster.

In this we Americans were discovering no wholly new truth; we were writing a new chapter in our book of self-government.

This year marks the one hundred and fiftieth anniversary of the Constitutional Convention which made us a nation. At that Convention our forefathers found the way out of the chaos which followed the Revolutionary War; they created a strong government with powers of united action sufficient then and now to solve problems utterly beyond individual or local solution. A century and a half ago they established the Federal Government in order to promote the general welfare and secure the blessings of liberty to the American people.

Today we invoke those same powers of government to achieve the same objectives.

Four years of new experience have not belied our historic instinct. They hold out the clear hope that government within communities, government within the separate States, and government of the United States can do the things the times require, without yielding its democracy. Our tasks in the last four years did not force democracy to
take a holiday.

Nearly all of us recognize that as intricacies of human relationships increase, so power to govern them also must increase—power to stop evil; power to do good. The essential democracy of our nation and the safety of our people depend not upon the absence of power, but upon lodging it with those whom the people can change or continue at stated intervals through an honest and free system of elections. The Constitution of 1787 did not make our democracy impotent.

In fact, in these last four years, we have made the exercise of all power more democratic; for we have begun to bring private autocratic powers into their proper subordination to the public's government. The legend that they were invincible—above and beyond the processes of a democracy—has been shattered. They have been challenged and beaten.

Source: Daley, James, ed. *Great Inaugural Addresses*. Mineola, NY: Dover Thrift Editions, 2010.

# 6.3 Charles I. Dawson: "The President Has Made the Issue" (1936)

## Document Overview

*Charles I. Dawson was a lawyer in Louisville, Kentucky, who was a member of the American Liberty League. The Liberty League was one of a few groups of particularly ardent New Deal opponents who based that opposition on what they perceived as Franklin Roosevelt's willingness to undermine American capitalism in general and the Constitution in particular. In this speech at the group's annual dinner, Dawson laid down a legal and philosophical case against the actions Roosevelt took during his first term, regardless of whatever help they offered to desperate Americans.*

## Document Text

When Mr. Roosevelt, as President, took the oath to support and defend the Constitution of the United States, he could look back at nearly one hundred and fifty years of National existence under that instrument. He is a lawyer, and we have the right to assume that he was thoroughly familiar with its provisions and with the interpretation and meaning given to those provisions by the Supreme Court of the United States.

He knew that the purpose of that instrument was not to record a grant of rights and privileges to its citizens by the National Government, but that on the contrary its purpose was to create a new National Government, and to specifically record the powers conferred upon that government by its creators—the people of the United States.

He knew, by the terms of the instrument itself and from an unbroken line of opinions from the Supreme Court, that the only powers possessed by the National Government are those expressly or impliedly conferred upon it by that Constitution.

He knew that the constitution was framed and adopted by men who were proudly conscious of the fact that they were citizens of independent sovereign states, and that by creating the National Government, they had no intention of surrendering into the keeping of the new government those inalienable rights which the Declaration of Independence declares are the heritage of all free men; that among these inalienable rights are the right to life, liberty and the pursuit of happiness; the right to labor in lawful occupations of their own choosing, free of government interference and to enjoy the fruits of their labor; to acquire and hold property and be assured of its protection, not only against spoliation by the Government, but against the avarice and designs of their fellow-men.

He knew that those who framed the Constitution had no intention of destroying their respective state governments, or of surrendering any of the powers of the state governments to the National Government, except to the extent and in the manner set out in the Constitution itself.

He knew that there was conferred upon the National Government no power of control over the internal affairs of the state; no power to regulate the farm, the factory, the mill or the mine.

He knew that the National Government has no power to take the property of any citizen, or group of citizens, whether under the guise of taxation or through condemnation, for the benefit of any other citizen or group of citizens.

He knew that the Constitution confers upon the National Government no police power within the respective states, under which Congress may legislate for what it conceives to be the general welfare, it matters not how grave the emergency nor how great the demand for such legislation may be.

Source: Dawson, Charles I. "The President Has Made the Issue." American Liberty League, 1936.

# 6.4 Questions

1. Describe the differences in philosophy between Roosevelt and Dawson about the role of the federal government in American life. Who is right (both legally and ethically)?

2. Would Roosevelt agree with Dawson that his conception of the New Deal marks a break with how the framers of the Constitution imagined the federal government acting in times of emergency? Explain in reference to Roosevelt's speech.

3. Assuming Dawson is correct about how the framers of the Constitution saw the role of the federal government, does the existence of an economic emergency justify changing that role? Explain.

# 7.1 Segregation in the North and South

## Introduction

Jim Crow segregation developed in the South in the last decades of the nineteenth century as a way for racist white people to reestablish the social control that they once had during slavery. Sometimes it was written into law, but often it was perpetuated entirely through social customs. While the South tended to rely on laws to impose segregation (which were ruled constitutional by the Supreme Court's infamous 1896 *Plessy v. Ferguson* decision), the northern states that imposed segregation tended to depend upon custom.

The imposition of segregation outside the South was inconsistent, which tended to make it more unpredictable. This was particularly true in the North, where the existence of segregation is not always recognized since it was implemented in a more subtle manner. While not perhaps directly in dialogue, these documents offer two different kinds of solutions to the same problem.

# 7.2 W.E.B. Du Bois: "Segregation in the North" (1934)

## Document Overview

*The civil rights leader W.E.B Du Bois recommended an uncompromising stand against segregation no matter how it was implemented, suggesting that African Americans like him should organize against the strictures imposed against them even if some African Americans still benefited by selling products and services to the trapped inhabitants of segregated neighborhoods. This document was the draft for an article intended to be published in* The Crisis, *the official magazine of the NAACP.*

## Document Text

The difference between North and South in the matter of segregation is larges a difference of degree, if we accept the prevalence of mob law and political and social disenfranchisement in the South. In the North, [a]nyone with a feasible admixture of Negro blood [cannot] frequent hotels or restaurants. They have difficulty finding dwelling places in white neighborhoods. ... Their children either go to colored schools or to schools nominally for both races, but actually attended almost exclusively by colored children. In other words, they are confined by unyielding public opinion to a Negro world. And no matter how much they may fulminate about no segregation, there stand the flat facts. Moreover, this situation has been steadily growing worse. ...

What then can we do? The only thing that we not only can but must do is to organize our economic and social power. Remember to associate with ourselves and train ourselves for executive association. Organize our consuming strength. Train ourselves in methods of democracy. Run our own institutions. We are doing this partially now, only we are doing it under a peculiar attitude of protest. ... Segregation may be compulsory by law, or it may be compulsory by economic or social condition. Or it may be a matter of free choice. At any rate, it is the separation of people. And that separation is evil and leads to nationalism and war, and yet it is today inevitable. Inevitable because without it the American Negro and other world groups would suffer evils greater than the evils of separation. They would suffer the loss of self-respect, the lack of faith in themselves, the lack of knowledge about themselves, the lack of ability to make a decent living.

Source: Du Bois, W.E.B. "Segregation in the North." *Crisis* (April 1934).

# 7.3 Victor H. Green: The Negro Motorist "Green Book" (1940)

## Document Overview

*Victor H. Green, in his periodical the* Green Book *(which was both the color green and named after him), provided African Americans a way to circumvent the strictures of segregation in both northern and southern states by finding restaurants, hotels, and sometimes even private homes that were willing to serve them despite the limitations imposed by informal segregation. While his book consisted of nothing but a list of places, the Introduction to the 1940 edition makes it clear that Green was engaged in an early form of crowdsourcing.*

## Document Text

INTRODUCTION

The idea of "The Green Book" is to give the Motorist and Tourist a Guide not only of the Hotels and Tourist Homes in all of the large cities, but other classifications that will be found useful wherever he may be. Also facts and information that the Negro Motorist can use and depend upon.

There are thousands of places that the public doesn't know about and aren't listed. Perhaps you know of some? If so send in their names and addresses and the kind of business, so that we might pass it along to the rest of your fellow Motorists.

You will find it handy on your travels, whether at home or in some other state, and is up to date. Each year we are compiling new lists as some of these places move, or go out of business and new business places are started giving added employment to members of our race.

When you are traveling mention "The Green Book" so as to let these people know just how you found out about their place of business. If they haven't heard about This Guide, tell them to get in touch with us.

If this Guide is useful, let us know, if not tell us also, as we appreciate your criticisms.

If any errors are found, kindly notify the publishers so that they can be corrected in the next issue.

Published yearly in the month of April by Victor H. Green.

Source: Green, Victor H. *The Negro Motorist Green-Book*. New York: Victor H. Green, 1940.

## 7.4 Questions

1. Both these documents acknowledge the existence of segregation in the North during this era, but how do they differ in suggestions of how to combat it?

2. What "economic and social power" (in the words of Du Bois) did African Americans have during segregation? How do these varying responses to segregation in the North and South demonstrate that power?

3. Is any kind of compromise with evil inherently suspect? In other words, is working around segregation just another way of accepting it?

# 8.1 Anti-Communism

## Introduction

The American Communist Party formed in 1919. It grew during the Great Depression but lost members in the years preceding World War II because so many American communists were disgusted by the rule of Soviet leader Josef Stalin. As a result, the vast majority of Americans were not communists during the post-World War II years. They hated and feared this ideology. Nevertheless, Americans grew very afraid of communists in their midst during the post-war years. The question to consider here is why.

While some institutions seemed truly scared by the potential that a small minority of communists could somehow trick their fellow citizens into giving up their liberties, others believed that American institutions would keep the American democratic political system intact despite the threat that communism posed. While anti-communists of all kinds greatly exaggerated the threat that communism posed inside the United States, their attitudes towards that threat reveal much about the state of anxiety that pervaded America during this era.

# 8.2 Chamber of Commerce of the United States: "Communist Infiltration in the United States: Its Nature and How to Combat It" (1946)

## Document Overview

*The United States Chamber of Commerce, a business advocacy group that originated in 1912, embraced anti-communism during the Cold War years because its members felt threatened by the existence of anti-capitalist sentiments around the world. Having thrived during two world wars, American businesses wanted to expand internationally. These businesses required political support for that expansion from American citizens to get the federal government to protect their interests worldwide. By labeling its political enemies as communists and trying to persuade the noncommitted that the chamber's interests were identical to American interests, this section of a 1946 Chamber of Commerce leaflet illustrates the manner in which American business helped bring the Cold War to the home front.*

## Document Text

### Why Do People Become Communists?

The [Communist] system just described seems so fantastic to most Americans that it is almost incredible. Indeed, the Canadian investigating commission was hard put to explain why so many citizens professed a higher loyalty to a political power outside their borders. In fact, the motivation of Communists and their followers is extremely complex and unless this fact is recognized, countermeasures are likely to be ineffective.

With a few, it is a perverted form of idealism, a worldly substitute for religion. Some people are personally maladjusted and are chronic rebels. The Communist movement gives them an outlet. Many became Communists as a reaction against abuses in the present social and political order. In particular, many Communists are rebels against one or another form of exploitation. In certain cases, their conversion may be traced to some bitter experience in the labor field. Others may have felt discrimination because they were members of minority groups. To such persons, Communism is preached as a doctrine which promises equality to all.

Many intellectuals have been won over to Communism on the basis of rosy accounts of life in the Soviet Union. These persons are well aware of the faults in our own system, and have been led to believe that in Russia none of these evils exists. When the faults of Communism are called to their attention, they either dismiss the charges as capitalist propaganda or else consider them as transitional evils to be overlooked in the great promise of the future. The urge to remake the world is strong among some intellectuals. Some are sufficiently detached from everyday life to be indifferent to the cruel sufferings of the so-called transitional period.

Other motives are less creditable. Some individuals in civic and labor politics appreciate the support of a disciplined minority. They know the value of the publicity which it affords. Such persons follow the Party for motives of expediency rather than conviction. In other cases, vanity may suffice. This is particularly true of specialists who feel their inadequacy in broader affairs. A scientist or a motion picture star is often highly flattered in being asked to address a political meeting. In Hollywood, Communists arranged a meeting peopled by motion picture stars and scientists, each group attracted by the prospect of meeting the other. This technique of using celebrities is widely practiced.

Finally, many liberals follow the Communist line through confused good will. As one writer put it, some persons are so busy doing good that they fail to realize the harm their efforts cause. These are the "joiners," who readily give their names to any organization whose apparent purpose is noble. Thus the president of a great State university has become affiliated with some twenty such "fronts." Actually, in scores of cases such names and money are used to promote Communist causes. The Party has even enlisted persons of wealth to support its causes through the medium of these "front" groups. Even a casual study of the power and influence of Communist "fronts" should dispel the notion that the Party is weak and ineffectual.

Source: *Investigation of Un-American Propaganda Activities in the United States: Hearings before the Committee of Un-American Activities House of Representatives Eightieth Congress First Session on H.R. 1884 and H.R. 2122.* Washington, DC: United States Government Printing Office, 1947.

# 8.3 Ryland W. Crary and Gerald L. Steibel: "How You Can Teach About Communism" (1951)

## Document Overview

*Throughout the early Cold War years, many devout anti-communists felt the need to offer long explanations as to why the Western democratic system of government was superior to communism. Unlike the men who ran the Chamber of Commerce, they felt that a better understanding of American institutions was vital to combatting communism so that citizens would not be fooled by the false promises of communist leaders. Ryland W. Crary and Gerald L. Steibel were a professor of history and a psychological warfare officer with the U.S. Army, respectively. This introduction to their guide for social studies teachers demonstrates their faith in the intrinsic superiority of the American system, no matter how sneaky the communists happened to be.*

## Document Text

You can't teach about democracy unless you can cope with totalitarian propaganda—not with parroted cliches and easy phrases, but with realistic answers, framed in a democratic context.

We've never heard anyone dispute this assumption. But ...

Few teachers colleges offer any systematic instruction dealing with Russia or Communist ideology. Less than five percent of students graduating from teachers colleges have been enrolled in such courses.

If ignorance was our best defense against Communism, we would be well bolstered indeed. But ignorance is never an answer. If public education is to serve the democracy which produced it, it must provide students with a clear understanding of the realities of the present-day struggle. Teachers must know the facts and know how to teach them.

What are these facts? Primarily, they are those which have to do with Marxism and Russian history, with Russia's resources and political institutions, her cultural and educational life. The public school teacher needs to know the facts which illustrate why Communists are antithetic to the democratic way of life; why Communism has had appeal for hungry, frustrated, or embittered people.

But it is not enough for the teacher to know the facts about Communism, to know about what he is against. He must know what he is for, and be able to state his knowledge with eloquence and conviction. He must be helped to appreciate and understand the democratic tradition, to know what is meant by free intelligence, free inquiry, free dissent, free choice—all of which are rooted out under Communism. Communism has to be met and defeated on whatever ground it seeks to occupy.

The teacher in a democracy can certainly take the offensive, too. He can ask challenging questions of the Communist, questions such as: "What kind of individual does your authoritarian education produce?" "What is happening to creativity in arts and sciences in Russia?" "Where are your free workers and their right to strike?" . . .

We must recognize that there is too little time to teach all the fascinating lore in the world. We have to omit certain things of lesser historical significance than those events affecting the great crisis of our mid-century. It is simply bad judgment on the part of a history teacher if his students learn a good deal about ancient Egypt and Babylon, and little but a common stock of misapprehensions and errors about modern Russia and China.

The American history course should also include more material to help build understanding of America's role in the mid-twentieth century world. It is critically important that we study our record of foreign relations and understand our attitude toward other peoples and other nations. It is just as important, in American history, that we know what other people have thought of us and our actions at particular periods.

Source: Crary, Ryland Wesley. *How You Can Teach about Communism*. New York: Anti-defamation League of B'nai B'rith, 1951.

## 8.4 Questions

1. Did America really have anything to fear from communism during the post-World War II era? Could communists have really taken over our entire society despite their tiny numbers?

2. Who were the audiences for these respective documents? Did that do anything to determine the approach towards the communist threat recommended by their authors?

3. Should history really be applied to current political problems, as Crary and Steibel's approach suggests? Why or why not?

# 9.1 The Modern Women's Movement

## Introduction

In the years preceding women's suffrage, women of all classes could agree on an urgent need for women to be able to vote, since this was an obvious prerequisite for any kind of political power. Once they achieved that goal, the goal of women involved in politics splintered. Women's involvement in the workplace during World War II interested many women in achieving economic equality. Other women gained experience in politics through their involvement with the civil rights movement during the 1950s and 1960s.

The modern women's rights movement started in the late-1960s, and almost immediately it inspired participants who favored different approaches. On the one hand, young radicals who had cut their teeth fighting for African American civil rights earlier in the decade came to believe that far-reaching change required a huge alteration in American culture. These radicals were willing to fight for that change even if it was not immediately popular. On the other hand, older women and single professional women tended to focus their efforts on using changes in the law like the passage of the Civil Rights Act of 1964 to improve the pay and employment conditions of women in the workplace. While these two positions were by no means mutually exclusive, the differences in approach mark a key division that persisted throughout this movement during its most influential years.

# 9.2 Casey Hayden and Mary King: "Sex and Caste" (1965)

## Document Overview

*Casey Hayden and Mary King were two of many women working in the civil rights movement for African Americans in the South during the early 1960s. Over time, they became dissatisfied by how they were treated, and by how the overwhelmingly male leadership of that movement treated women in general, relegating them to support roles and preventing them from becoming involved in making important decisions. Their memo "Sex and Caste" is not only a key document of that effort, it is perhaps the best illustration possible of how one social movement for civil rights—the campaign on behalf of African Americans—led directly to another—the feminist movement of the late 1960s and 1970s.*

## Document Text

Sex and caste: There seem to be many parallels that can be drawn between treatment of Negroes and treatment of women in our society as a whole. But in particular, women we've talked to who work in the movement seem to be caught up in a common-law caste system that operates, sometimes subtly, forcing them to work around or outside hierarchical structures of power which may exclude them. Women seem to be placed in the same position of assumed subordination in personal situations too. It is a caste system which, at its worst, uses and exploits women....

The caste system perspective dictates the roles assigned to women in the movement, and certainly even more to women outside the movement. Within the movement, questions arise in situations ranging from relationships of women organizers to men in the community, to who cleans the freedom house, to who holds leadership positions, to who does secretarial work, and who acts as spokesman for groups. Other problems arise between women with varying degrees of awareness of themselves as being as capable as men but held back from full participation, or between women who see themselves as needing more control of their work than other women demand. And there are problems with relationships between white women and black women. . . .

Having learned from the movement to think radically about the personal worth and abilities of people whose role in society had gone unchallenged before, a lot of women in the movement have begun trying to apply those lessons to their own relations with men. Each of us probably has her own story of the various results, and of the internal struggle occasioned by trying to break out of very deeply learned fears, needs, and self-perceptions, and of what happens when we try to replace them with concepts of people and freedom learned from the movement and organizing. . . .

Objectively, the chances seem nil that we could start a movement based on anything as distant to general American thought as a sex caste system. Therefore, most of us will probably want to work full time on problems such as war, poverty, race. The very fact that the country can't face, much less deal with, the questions we're raising means that the movement is one place to look for some relief.

Source: Hayden, Casey and Mary King. "Sex and Caste: A Kind of Memo." *Liberation* 10 (April 1966): 35-36.

# 9.3 Betty Friedan: Commencement Speech to Smith College Graduates (1981)

## Document Overview

*Betty Friedan first came to public attention for writing the book* The Feminine Mystique, *a national best-seller upon its publication in 1963. The book was an examination of how her classmates at Smith College, an all-female school in Northampton, Massachusetts, had fared in life during the prosperous post-World War II era. Their dissatisfaction, and the letters she received from other women who read her book, helped inspire Friedan to co-found the National Organization for Women (NOW) in 1966. When she returned to give the Smith College commencement speech to graduates in 1981, the feminist movement had become part of the American mainstream.*

## Document Text

The reality of intelligent Smith women that were housewives was very different from that denigrating image, but there is no way that women today, for reasons of economic survival of families if nothing else, can return to even play-acting a dependent, subservient, passive role of housewife, where woman is quote-unquote "just a housewife," where she is defined in terms solely as man's wife, children's mother, server of physical needs of husband, children and home. That image that defined and confined our image, our possibilities, our potential energies, nearly twenty years ago when I gave it the term *The Feminine Mystique.*

But we have to beware of being locked in a reactionary feminist mystique. Feminism—the gut reality of mainstream feminism—has opened life and the possibility of life for women, men and children, but the reality of feminism in no way is opposed to the family.

In the first stage, the very ability of women to work outside the home and get a decent wage and get access to professions—whether women were housewives, whether women were working outside the home—was held back by that image of woman, the feminine mystique, that defined women solely in terms of the passive, subservient housewife role in the family.

Our thrust in the first stage of feminism had to be on the personhood of women and on breaking through the barriers, the simple barriers if you will, of sex discrimination in the society as well as those barriers as we interjected them in our own consciousness that kept us from moving as people in our own right and fully demanding the equality of opportunity that was our human birthright, our American birthright.

That feminine mystique—we had to get rid of it, we had to break through it, we had to break through the limitation to affirm our personhood of woman. And the thrust was on the things that we did as individuals, as individuals, in professions, in all that field outside the home that had been called and defined "man's world" and where women moved only as exceptions and freaks did the menial housework.

We had to make ourselves visible out of that world. We had to break through the barriers. We had to uncover all the buried history, the double standards that existed when women were invisible as people in that world.

But there was a danger. There was a slight danger and the media exaggerated it, but some of our own ideological mistakes in our own rhetoric carried the danger, too, of a reaction so strong against the feminine mystique that, if you will, that there was a tendency to throw out some of the baby off with the bathwater—just throw out a little bit. That from being defined solely in terms of an obsolete, narrow definition of woman's role that wasn't really possible to live in the new 80-year lifespan and in the new economic demands of society.

Even if we were still living in terms of families facing choices and decisions about children in existing marriages or facing questions about marriages, our consciousness—the part of it that we termed as feminism—focused on these other questions.

And then there came to be the image that somehow feminism against the family, as if a narrow definition of feminism, family didn't belong. And then this played into reaction. For reaction took some ideological mistake or ideological oversimplification that seemed right for awhile. They sounded revolutionary. They expressed our anger. . . .

Today, I am concerned with our ability—with your ability—to live that equality and to preserve it. We have to realize that if we replace a feminine mystique which denied, ignored, did not allow us to think in terms of the aspirations and the potentials of women which are not defined by her role as wife and mother, if we replace that by a feminist mystique that denies the aspects and attributes of the personhood of women that through the ages have been expressed in nurture—our own needs to love and be loved, the realities of family which are the human nutrient for us all—we shortchange ourselves, our potential, our personhood as women.

Source: Friedan, Betty. "Commencement Speech to Smith College Graduates." Iowa State University, Carrie Chapman Catt Center for Women and Politics. https://awpc.cattcenter.iastate.edu/2018/10/12/smith-college-commencement-address-may-24-1981/.

## 9.4 Questions

1. Why did Hayden and King decide they had to critique the actions of people who were nominally part of the same movement as they were?

2. Where do Hayden and King's ideas fit into Friedan's conception of the stages of the feminist movement?

3. Which of these two approaches has had the greatest effect upon the lives of women down to today? Explain.

# 10.1 The Generation Gap and the Vietnam War

## Introduction

The Vietnam War can be traced back to World War II, when Vietnamese nationalists recognized that their French colonial rulers were weak enough to be defeated. Americans first became involved in this struggle as the French lost interest in fighting to keep control of this distant possession. American interest in Vietnam was primarily a product of the global Cold War against communism rather than the resources available in that area. American presidents from Harry Truman onward were desperate to keep Vietnam from falling under communist control for domestic political reasons.

"The Generation Gap" was a phrase used during the 1960s that represented the difference between young Baby Boomers and their parents about many aspects of American life, but it was particularly apt for describing differences of opinion over the Vietnam War. Parents who came of age during the height of the Cold War remained susceptible to politicians invoking the dangers of communism in situations where the communist threat to the United States was distant at best, while young people who were just becoming politically aware had developed an entirely different set of priorities. These speeches about the Vietnam War by the president of the United States and an anti-war protestor reflect that generation gap in that they invoke entirely different sets of priorities, despite being about the exact same subject.

# 10.2 Lyndon B. Johnson: "Peace without Conquest" Speech about Vietnam (1965)

## Document Overview

*Lyndon Johnson inherited the Vietnam War from his predecessor, John F. Kennedy, who in turn inherited the war from Dwight D. Eisenhower. There was a political consensus, regardless of party, that any country around the world that fell to communism, no matter how small and insignificant, represented a defeat for the United States because of the effect that it would have on America's international reputation. Johnson's problem was that as South Vietnam, which had become a client state of the United States, became increasingly unstable, it required more economic and military aid, as well as American troops, to keep that country from falling to communist insurgents supported by the Soviet client state in North Vietnam. By 1965, when he gave this address at Johns Hopkins University, Johnson had to make the case to the American people in the starkest possible terms in order to flag up wavering support for the war at home.*

## Document Text

... Over this war—and all Asia—is another reality: the deepening shadow of Communist China. The rulers in Hanoi are urged on by Peking. This is a regime which has destroyed freedom in Tibet, which has attacked India, and has been condemned by the United Nations for aggression in Korea. It is a nation which is helping the forces of violence in almost every continent. The contest in Vietnam is part of a wider pattern of aggressive purposes.

Why are these realities our concern? Why are we in South Vietnam?

We are there because we have a promise to keep. Since 1954 every American President has offered support to the people of South Vietnam. We have helped to build, and we have helped to defend. Thus, over many years, we have made a national pledge to help South Vietnam defend its independence.

And I intend to keep that promise.

To dishonor that pledge, to abandon this small and brave nation to its enemies, and to the terror that must follow, would be an unforgivable wrong.

We are also there to strengthen world order. Around the globe, from Berlin to Thailand, are people whose well-being rests, in part, on the belief that they can count on us if they are attacked. To leave Viet-Nam to its fate would shake the confidence of all these people in the value of an American commitment and in the value of America's word. The result would be increased unrest and instability, and even wider war.

We are also there because there are great stakes in the balance. Let no one think for a moment that retreat from Viet-Nam would bring an end to conflict. The battle would be renewed in one country and then another. The central lesson of our time is that the appetite of aggression is never satisfied. To withdraw from one battlefield means only to prepare for the next. We must say in southeast Asia—as we did in Europe—in the words of the Bible: "Hitherto shalt thou come, but no further."

There are those who say that all our effort there will be futile—that China's power is such that it is bound to dominate all southeast Asia. But there is no end to that argument until all of the nations of Asia are swallowed up.

There are those who wonder why we have a responsibility there. Well, we have it there for the same reason that we have a responsibility for the defense of Europe. World War II was fought in both Europe and Asia, and when it ended we found ourselves with continued responsibility for the defense of freedom.

Our objective is the independence of South Viet-Nam, and its freedom from attack. We want nothing for ourselves—only that the people of South Viet-Nam be allowed to guide their own country in their own way.

We will do everything necessary to reach that objective. And we will do only what is absolutely necessary....

Source: Johnson, Lyndon B. "Peace without Conquest." In *Supplemental Foreign Assistance, Fiscal Year 1996—Vietnam: Hearings before the Committee on Foreign Relations, United States Senate, Eighty-Ninth Congress, Second Session on S. 2793, to Amend Further the Foreign Assistance Act of 1961, as Amended, Part 1*. Washington, DC: U.S. Government Printing Office, 1966.

# 10.3 Raymond Anthony Mungo: Anti-War Speech (1967)

## Document Overview

*Raymond Mungo was a student leader at Boston College when he gave this speech at an anti-war rally on Boston Common. He would go on to be a journalist and a leader in the back-to-the-land movement, one of many subgroups of the larger 1960s counterculture dedicated to reversing the excesses of the modern world. This particular speech is no different than many other speeches given at many other anti-war rallies of the Vietnam era, but the transcript of this one ended up in the U.S. National Archives because it was recorded without his knowledge by the Boston Police Department. In the speech, Mungo told the crowd that he was resisting the draft, which meant that the police tape of the speech could have been used as evidence for his prosecution.*

## Document Text

In 1965 I was aware of the war in Vietnam. I burned my draft card on the 20th anniversary of the bombing of Hiroshima. In 1967, I'm here today, and this is a very historic day, to go with you to the Arlington Street Church, to say to you that I have nothing . . . more to do with the Selective Service System. . . . I do not believe . . . that it's a coincidence that the United states Army, that the same United States Army that's destroying people in Vietnam, can be destroying people in Detroit. I think that it's connected. I think people who go to fight and kill people find it easier to come back here and kill people, and I think killing people is wrong in any situation, because people is all that we have. . . .

I might be crazy. Why am I subjecting myself to the possibility of jail? Why do I not sit and accept the arguments that many political activists have offered me, that it is more effective to stay out of jail and play along with the system? Because you can't revolutionize the system and you can't change a country that is rotten to the core unless you make a complete break. I

cannot object to American materialism if I depend on American affluence and I'm afraid of jail. I am not afraid of jail. I'm afraid of killing people and being killed and I'm afraid the whole planet is going up in smoke if we don't do something about it immediately. Jail is not to be feared. Jail is an honorable alternative to this
war in Vietnam....

If resisting the Government in the United States of America, which is killing people abroad and killing people at home, black people and yellow people and poor people, if that is treason, I want to be a traitor. I want to be nothing but a traitor. It's the only honorable thing to be, and I want as many of you as are ready to take this step today to come with me and a lot of other people down to the Arlington Street Church to tell the United States Government together, today, that you are men, and not tools, that you have rights and you have dignity and that you belong to the human race. That's all I'm asking you to do.

Source: Mungo, Raymond Anthony. "Anti-War Speech." Boston Common, 1928-1976; Precedent Case Files, 1928 -1976; Records of U.S. Attorneys, Record Group 118; National Archives at Boston, Waltham, MA.

## 10.4 Questions

1. How did Johnson try to make the case that Americans had a direct interest in the fate of South Vietnam? Did he do a good job? Why or why not?

2. Was the freedom of South Vietnam worth the cost that the United States paid in the blood of its citizens? Explain.

3. Do you find Mungo's argument persuasive? Why or why not?

# II.1 The Gay Rights Movement

## Introduction

The gay rights movement was inspired by the African American civil rights movement of the 1950s and 1960s. Its roots are generally traced to the Stonewall Riots of 1969, and in some ways it has been even more successful than the fight for racial equality. From often hiding their true selves from their families (not to mention society at large), gay people have achieved enormous societal acceptance over the last half century, best symbolized by the Supreme Court's decision in *Obergefell v. Hodges* in 2015, which required all fifty states to accept same-sex marriages.

Despite this success, gay rights activists have faced enormous amounts of resistance in their path to the societal mainstream. While it is historically important to understand the roots of prejudice of all kinds, to describe it here at a juncture when this battle for civil rights remains active would only encourage prejudice. Therefore, these documents are more about strategies towards achieving acceptance than they are about two opposing sides of a morality debate in which society has begun to leave the opposition behind.

# 11.2 Anita Bryant Is Hit by a Pie (1977)

## Document Overview

*Anita Bryant was gospel singer, spokeswoman for Florida Orange Juice, and anti-gay activist during the 1970s. She was a driving force behind a campaign to repeal a gay civil rights ordinance passed in Dade County, Florida, in 1977. In October 1977 gay rights activist Tom Higgins threw a pie in her face during a press conference she gave in Des Moines, Iowa. The following is a transcript of what transpired.*

## Document Text

Bryant is surprised by pie thrown in her face.

*Bryant:* "At least it's a fruit pie."

*Unidentified Man Next to Bryant:* "Let's pray for him right now. Anita. Anita, why don't you pray."

*Bryant:* "Father, we want to thank you for the opportunity of coming to Des Moines. And father I want to ask that you forgive him."

*Unidentified Man:* "And that we love him."

*Bryant:* "And that we love him. And that we're praying for him [crying] to be delivered from his deviant lifestyle. Father, and I just ... [crying]."

*Unidentified Man:* "We forgive you. We love you. I don't want this man touched or harmed in any way.... You have done your cause more harm"

*Higgins:* "Thus always to bigots."

*Unidentified Man:* "Do you know who's here? Do you know [who] saw you do that?"

*Higgins:* "Thus always to bigots...."

*Unidentified Man:* "This man is from *Rolling Stone* magazine. Do you know what kind of publicity you're going to get?"

*Higgins:* "I can't stand the garbage you spout...."

*Bryant [tasting pie]:* "It's not bad."

Source: https://www.youtube.com/watch?v=5tHGmSh7f-0

# 11.3 Harvey Milk: Gay Freedom Day Speech (1978)

## Document Overview

*San Francisco elected Harvey Milk to its Board of Supervisors in 1977, just a few short years after he had moved there from New York. Milk was representative of many gay and bisexual people who moved to San Francisco because of its climate of openness and tolerance. He was San Francisco's first openly gay politician and at that time easily the most important gay political figure in the United States.*

*Milk and San Francisco Mayor George Moscone were assassinated in November 1978. Before that, Milk expressed his ideas about how gay people could achieve equality at a mass rally in front of San Francisco City Hall on Gay Freedom Day in June 1978.*

## Document Text

My name is Harvey Milk and I'm here to recruit you. I've been saying this one for years. It's a political joke. I can't help it—I've got to tell it. I've never been able to talk to this many political people before, so if I tell you nothing else you may be able to go home laughing a bit....

In 1977, gay people had their rights taken away from them in Miami. But you must remember that in the week before Miami and the week after that, the word homosexual or gay appeared in every single newspaper in this nation in articles both pro and con. In every radio station, in every TV station and every household. For the first time in the history of the world, everybody was talking about it, good or bad. Unless you have dialogue, unless you open the walls of dialogue, you can never reach to change people's opinion. In those two weeks, more good and bad, but more about the word homosexual and gay was written than probably in the history of mankind. Once you have dialogue starting, you know you can break down prejudice....

... Gay people have been slandered nationwide. We've been tarred and we've been brushed with the picture of pornography. In Dade County, we were accused of child molestation. It's not enough anymore just to have friends represent us. No matter how good that friend may be.

The black community made up its mind to that a long time ago. That the myths against blacks can only be dispelled by electing black leaders, so the black community could be judged by the leaders and not by the myths or black criminals. The Spanish community must not be judged by Latin criminals or myths. The Asian community must not be judged by Asian criminals or myths. The Italian community must not be judged by the mafia, myths. And the time has come when the gay community must not be judged by our criminals and myths.

Like every other group, we must be judged by our leaders and by those who are themselves gay, those who are visible. For invisible, we remain in limbo—a myth, a person with no parents, no brothers, no sisters, no friends who are straight, no important positions in employment. A tenth of the nation supposedly composed of stereotypes and would-be seducers of children—and no offense meant to the stereotypes. But today, the black community is not judged by its friends, but by its black legislators and leaders. And we must give people the chance to judge us by our leaders and legislators. A gay person in office can set a tone, con command respect not only from the larger community, but from the young people in our own community who need both examples and hope.

The first gay people we elect must be strong. They must not be content to sit in the back of the bus. They must not be content to accept pablum. They must be above wheeling and dealing. They must be—for the good of all of us—independent, unbought. The anger and the frustrations that some of us feel is because we are misunderstood, and friends can't feel the anger and frustration. They can sense it in us, but they can't feel it. Because a friend has never gone through what is known as coming out. I will never forget what it was like coming out and having nobody to look up toward. I remember the lack of hope—and our friends can't fulfill it.

I can't forget the looks on faces of people who've lost hope. Be they gay, be they seniors, be they blacks looking for an almost-impossible job, be they Latins trying to explain their problems and aspirations in a tongue that's foreign to them. I personally will never forget that people are more important than buildings. I use the word "I" because I'm proud. I stand here tonight in front of my gay sisters, brothers and friends because I'm proud of you. I think it's time that we have many legislators who are gay and proud of that fact and do not have to remain in the closet. I think that a gay person, up-front, will not walk away from a responsibility and be afraid of being tossed out of office. After Dade County, I walked among the angry and the frustrated night after night and I looked at their faces. And in San Francisco, three days before Gay Pride Day, a person was killed just because he was gay. And that night, I walked among the sad and the frustrated at City Hall in San Francisco and later that night as they lit candles on Castro Street and stood in silence, reaching out for some symbolic thing that would give them hope. These were strong people, whose faces I knew from the shop, the streets, meetings and people who I never saw before but I knew. They were strong, but even they needed hope.

And the young gay people in the Altoona, Pennsylvanias, and the Richmond, Minnesotas, who are coming out and hear Anita Bryant on television and her story. The only thing they have to look forward to is hope. And you have to give them hope. Hope for a better world, hope for a better tomorrow, hope for a better place to come to if the pressures at home are too great. Hope that all will be all right. Without hope, not only gays, but the blacks, the seniors, the handicapped, the us'es, the us'es will give up. And if you help elect to the central committee and other offices, more gay people, that gives a green light to all who feel disenfranchised, a green light to move forward.

It means hope to a nation that has given up, because if a gay person makes it, the doors are open to everyone.

Source: Milk, Harvey. "Gay Freedom Day Speech." June 25, 1978. https://www.archivesfoundation.org/amendingamerica/speech-san-francisco-supervisor-harvey-milk-gay-freedom-day-june-25-1978/.

## 11.4 Questions

1. Which tactics were better, Higgins's or Milk's?

2. Was Bryant's companion right about the effect of the press upon Higgins's action or was Milk? For gay rights, was there such a thing as bad publicity?

3. How did Higgins's and Milk's very different efforts complement each other?

4. How much of that success depended upon the prejudice of their opponents?

5. What does the ultimate success of the gay rights movement have to teach other social movements of today?

# 12.1 Globalization and the North American Free Trade Agreement

## Introduction

The North American Free Trade Agreement (NAFTA) was the first of a series of regionally based global trade treaties that lowered or eliminated tariffs for the United States and its trade partners around the world. Originally proposed by President George H.W. Bush, the treaty found support from his Democratic opponent in the 1992 election, Bill Clinton, as part of the latter's effort to depict himself as more moderate than his party's other recent presidential nominees.

While the details of the treaty were complicated, these speeches before and against reflect the economic philosophy of the politicians who gave them more so than the treaty itself. For most Americans, which philosophy they most agree with probably reflects whether they are a producer or a consumer of the goods being traded as much as it reflects their political affiliation. President Donald Trump subsequently spoke against NAFTA many times before and after becoming president, but many other Republicans have been reluctant to significantly revise the treaty, since they support its overall objectives of increased commerce no matter what the effects on domestic labor and manufacturing.

# 12.2 Ross Perot at the Third Presidential Debate (1992)

## Document Overview

*While Governor Bill Clinton supported the agreement that President George H.W. Bush negotiated during the 1992 presidential campaign, businessman Ross Perot in large part became an independent candidate for president during that race in large part to oppose the agreement. While there is debate over whether Perot's famous warning about a "giant sucking sound" eventually happened, there is no question that many displaced American workers realized the importance of this agreement to their economic lives only in hindsight.*

## Document Text

You implement that NAFTA, the Mexican trade agreement, where they pay people a dollar an hour, have no health care, no retirement, no pollution controls, et cetera, et cetera, et cetera, and you're going to hear a giant sucking sound of jobs being pulled out of this country right at a time when we need the tax base to pay the debt and pay down the interest on the debt and get our house back in order.

We've got to proceed very carefully on that. See, there's a lot I don't understand. I do understand business. I do understand creating jobs. I do understand how to make things work. And I got a long history of doing that.

Now, if you want to go to the core problem that faces everybody in manufacturing in this country, it's that agreement that's about to be put into practice. It's very simple. Everybody says it'll create jobs. Yes, it'll create bubble jobs.

Now, you know, watch this—listen very carefully to this. One-time surge while we build factories and ship machine tools and equipment down there. Then year after year for decades, they will have jobs. And I finally—I thought I didn't understand it—called all the experts, and they said, oh, it'll be disruptive for 12 to 15 years.

We haven't got 12 days, folks. We cannot lose those jobs. They were eventually saying, Mexican jobs will eventually come to $7.50 an hour, ours will eventually go down to $7.50 an hour. Makes you feel real good to hear that, right?

Let's think it through here. Let's be careful. I'm for free trade philosophically, but I have studied these trade agreements till the world has gone flat, and we don't have good trade agreements across the world.

Source: Debate Transcript, October 19, 1992. Commission on Presidential Debates. https://www.debates.org/voter-education/debate-transcripts/october-19-1992-debate-transcript/.

# 12.3 Bill Clinton: "Remarks on the Signing of NAFTA" (1993)

## Document Overview

*Bill Clinton's support for NAFTA during the 1992 presidential reflected his status as a new kind of Democrat. Ever since the New Deal of the 1930s, most Democrats had been extremely solicitous of the concerns of blue-collar workers and the unions that represented them. Clinton supported a treaty negotiated by a Republican president in large part to send a signal to businessmen that they had nothing to fear from his presidency. The fact that a Congress with a Democratic majority passed the treaty reflected his success at bringing the rest of the Democratic Party around to his ideas. The fact that the Democrats lost the majority of both houses of Congress in the next midterm election shows that the battle over the treaty left scars in the Democratic coalition that have not healed even today.*

## Document Text

In a few moments, I will sign the North American free trade act into law. NAFTA will tear clown trade barriers between our three nations. It will create the world's largest trade zone and create 200,000 jobs in this country by 1995 alone. The environmental and labor side agreements negotiated by our administration will make this agreement a force for social progress as well as economic growth. Already the confidence we've displayed by ratifying NAFTA has begun to bear fruit. We are now making real progress toward a worldwide trade agreement so significant that it could make the material gains of NAFTA for our country look small by comparison.

Today we have the chance to do what our parents did before us. We have the opportunity to remake the world. For this new era, our national security we now know will be determined as much by our ability to pull down foreign trade barriers as by our ability to breach distant ramparts. Once again, we are leading. And in so doing, we are rediscovering a fundamental truth about ourselves: When we lead, we build security, we build prosperity for our own people.

We've learned this lesson the hard way. Twice before in this century, we have been forced to define our role in the world. After World War I we turned inward, building walls of protectionism around our Nation. The result was a Great Depression and ultimately another horrible World War. After the Second World War, we took a different course: We reached outward. Gifted leaders of both political parties built a new order based on collective security and expanded trade. They created a foundation of stability and created in the process the conditions which led to the explosion of the great American middle class, one of the true economic miracles in the whole history of civilization. Their statecraft stands to this day: the IMF and the World Bank, GATT, and NATO. . . .

Make no mistake, the global economy with all of its promise and perils is now the central fact of life for hard-working Americans. It has enriched the lives of millions of Americans. But for too many those same winds of change have worn away at file basis of their security. For two decades, most people have worked harder for less. Seemingly secure jobs have been lost. And while America once again is the most productive nation on Earth, this productivity itself holds the seeds of further insecurity. After all, productivity means the same people can produce more or, very often, that fewer people can produce more. This is the world we face.

We cannot stop global change. We cannot repeal the international economic competition that is everywhere. We can only harness the energy to our benefit. Now we must recognize that the only way for a wealthy nation to grow richer is to export, to simply find new customers for the products and services it makes. That, my fellow Americans, is the decision the Congress made when they voted to ratify NAFTA.

Source: *Public Papers of the Presidents of the United States: William J. Clinton, 1993*. Book II. Washington, DC: United States Government Printing Office, 1994.

## 12.4 Questions

1. If we accept that NAFTA helped most Americans but hurt a few segments of the economy like organized labor, should those Americans have objected or stood down and let the treaty pass without opposition?

2. What should government do to help Americans hurt by wrenching economic changes like NAFTA?

3. Was President Clinton correct when he said, "We cannot stop global change"? Why or why not?

www.ingramcontent.com/pod-product-compliance
Lightning Source LLC
Chambersburg PA
CBHW052051300426
44117CB00012B/2082